"KEEP CLIMBING, EVEN IF YOU DON'T SEE THE TOP. JUST KNOW, THERE IS A TOP." JAMAR Q. CHILES

SHORT HILLS
&
TALL DREAMS

**Poems that will fortify your climb
to success and fortune**

Book and cover design by Jamar Q. Chiles

Printing and binding: 48 Hr Books Inc.

2249 14th St. SW

Akron OH 44314

ISBN 978-0-692-54924-7

To mom,
Who always tell
me what I try to
ignore.

Preface

"Short Hills & Tall Dreams," is a book of motivational poems that I wrote to encourage and keep peoples *DREAMS* and *GOALS* alive in a society governed by norms and expectations. Growing up in a single-parent home while living in Newark, NJ, an urban neighborhood surrounded with violence and temptation provided me with an alternative viewpoint that of the "average American family". My mom along with other family members and various people throughout my life instilled morals in me, and challenged me to overcome hardships and stigmas that the world provided to me since my very existence. As a child I was always intrigued by the way words made people feel and act. Whenever I heard a word that was unknown to me my inquisitive nature would always prompt me to find out it's meaning. Today I share my words that I learned and put together into poems and thoughts that will encourage you and allow you to tap into your various crafts. So I invite you to strap on your harness, open your mind, and prepare to climb this Short Hill to get to your Tall Dreams.

TABLE OF CONTENTS

<u>TITLE</u>   **PAGE**

TABLE OF CONTENTS

TITLE   **PAGE**

NOVEL (TODAY IS THE DAY)

Today is the day I am ready.
Today I will walk with my head high,
Today I will be brave, and won't cry.
Today I will finish yesterday's goals,
Today I will dig deep for spiritual gold.
Today I will face all of my fears,
Today I will fight all of my tears.
Today I will live like there's no tomorrow,
Today I will conquer all of my sorrows.
Today I will begin my new journey,
Today I will commence on my new story.
Today I will forget all of the hurt,
Today I will commit to life, and stop the
flirt.
Today is present for yesterday is the past,
Today is a new start, a brand new class.
Today is all we have because tomorrow
may never come,
Today is here and from today we cannot
run.

IN THE MASK

Take off your Mask and give it your all.
Let go of your fear and answer the call.
You can do it you, own your fate.
It may be tough but pick up the pace.
At times you may feel a little faint.
But don't hide your emotions with Mask paint.
Be you, and let your light shine.
Claim it, say it, "The Victory is mine.
If you are free of a Mask there is nothing to hide.
You will have more confidence the favor on your side.
Take off the Mask and show your face.
You can do it with wisdom and grace.
Once the Mask is off you will be free
I took my Mask off now look at me.

LIGHTS OUT

If the lights were out, we would all look
the same.
The only difference would be, our birth
giving names
You wouldn't see the color of my skin, or
the length of my hair.
You wouldn't even identify the clothes
that I wear.
If the lights were out, what would we
compare?
We would be so similar in all ways, if only
it were dark in here.
If the lights were out, what would we
judge; we would all be equal, if there
were no bulbs.
If the lights were out, we would all work
better together.
We would achieve many things to make
the world better.
 So why don't we vote and turn off the
lights.
Just know that the stars shine brighter
when it is night.

MIRROR

I want to be somebody, but I don't know
who.
 I want to be you, but you are you!
I want to be him, he's so cool.
I want to be her; she's such a jewel.
I want to be rich, I want the fame.
I want to be somebody, where everyone
knows my name.
I want to be popular, I want to be cute.
 I want to be anyone, that's worth the
hoot.
I want to be tall, just like a tree.
But one day I looked in the mirror, and I
realized that I was just fine being me.

WHO SAID

Those who said, "It couldn't be done,"
didn't do it.
Those who said, "You shouldn't try," they
already blew it.
Those who said, "You should settle,"
didn't move on.
Those who couldn't pick up the pieces,
wasn't strong.
Those who said, "stop!" didn't go.
Those who said, "The answer was
wrong," didn't know.
Those who said, "Give up," didn't try.
Those who didn't spread their wings
didn't fly.
Those who turned around, wasn't brave.
Those who went forward, the day was
saved.
Those who took the chance went far.
Success is near, and near you are.

HERE I STAND

I am somebody here I stand.
I have the ultimate master plan.
I must be respectful, learn all I can.
Knowledge is Power that will help me
grow into a great man.
I am somebody can you hear me?
My voice is low but high in quality.
I have a voice and a master plan.
I am somebody here I stand.
Here I stand, here I stand,
I am somebody here I stand.

LOSER

It's not always a bad thing to be a loser!
Lose your fear; lose your hate, Lose your
enemies, fresh new slate.
Lose your worries, lose your cares, Tackle
your goals, and lose your scares.
Lose low self-esteem give a smile.
Lose your baggage; you'll walk for miles.
Lose your doubts, lose your frowns, You
are royalty; here's your crown.
Lose your troubles, lose your tears, Lose
yourself in your dreams, and your—
Goals will find you there.
Lose the nervousness, lose being shy, Add
love to the mix, and you will fly! It's not
always a bad thing to...! Be a LOSER!

GO 4 IT

You miss all the goals that you don't take in life so....
Go 4 it!
If your scared to try it, try it, just....
Go 4 it!
What's it you wonder? It's your goals so...
Go 4 it!
Don't let it pass you by just....
Go 4 it!
The worst thing that can happen is that you did try so....
Go 4 it!
Imagine the success if you just....
Go 4 it!
You will be the best if you....
Go 4 it!
What are you waiting?
Go 4 it!
Go 4 it!
Go 4 it!

I WON'T GIVE UP

I won't give up, if the road is TOUGH!
I won't give up, if the battle is ROUGH!
I won't give up, no I will NOT!
I won't give up and I will not DROP!
I won't give up, because of my WILL
I won't give up, no, not STILL!
I won't give up, because I am STRONG!
I won't give up, because I BELONG!
I won't give up, there is light AHEAD!
I won't give up; I'm going to stick to what
I SAID!
I won't give up, I will get through THIS!
I won't give up, I will not MISS!
I won't give up, because I am BRAVE!
I won't give up, because success I
CRAVE!

I QUIT

I quit being angry and mad.
I quit being fearful, doubtful, and sad.
I quit being selfish, nervous and shy.
I quit being a victim and wondering why.
I quit living life regretting the past
I quit not being appreciative for all that I
have.
I quit walking out on challenges when
things don't go my way.
I am not a quitter but today is a new day.
I quit thinking negative and remembering
the hurt.
Today I quit negativity, now am alert.
I think positive which will attract better
days.
Negativity is now gone and I am no longer
it's slave.

TIME

Time keeps going, so use it wise.
Time is not guaranteed, it's life's prize.
Time is on no one's side and time we can't trust.
So take this time to write down your goals, it is a must.
Cause in no time it will be something that you wish you chose.
No one in history ever had a clock that froze.
So I say to you my friend as time goes on.
Tick Tock, Tick Tock—
Time so long.

BY THE CREEK

By the Creek is where I dream of success-
I write my goals and think the best.
By the Creek is where I reminisce-_
I think about the good times that I miss.
By the Creek is where I'm at peace--
At times It gets chilly so it's me my
thoughts and fleece.
By the Creek is where I get it done--
At heart I feel great, my feelings are
numb.
By the Creek is where it all makes sense--
So this is where I go when I'm tense.
By the Creek.

I MADE IT

I made it because of loving me.
I made it with a word that begins with the
letter D.
I made it because of dedication.
I made it because of determination.
I made it because I didn't give up.
I made it because my head stayed up.
I made it from retaining knowledge.
I made it and I will make it to college.
I made it, it didn't make I.
I made it because I kept my head high.
I made it because I conquered the heat.
I made it man victory is sweet.

TIME GOES ON

Sometimes you're on top,
Sometimes you're below.
Sometimes you have the answer,
sometimes you just don't know.
Sometimes you win,
Sometimes you lose.
Fate is half the choice the other half you
choose.
Sometimes you're ahead sometimes
you're behind.
Sometimes your failing but that's just
fine.
Failure just prepares you and puts you in
a positive win, win.
Just work through it and you will be on
top again.

DELAYED GRATI4CATION

Just because you don't hone it now--
doesn't mean you won't have it.
But when you do get close to it my friend
you just have to grab it.
Sometimes we don't get it immediately
because there is something better.
If you are in a storm right now, I'm here
to tell you that there is better weather.
Imagine the goal that you want and then
understand it.
You will then be able to execute the goal,
but don't forget to plan it.
One day my friend you will live out your
imagination.
Until then remember, Delayed
Grati4cation.

WISHING

You can sit there and wish for the world.
But wishing is nothing if your not
working.
Work toward your wish to make it come
true.
I will break it down just for you.
Work very hard and practice your craft.
Also be grateful and attentive with the
skills that you have.
Now you're working and wishing, wishing
and working.
Keep up the progress and your wish will
start working.
You can accomplish everything I believe
you can achieve it.
Stop wishing, start working and you will
receive it.

SUNDAY BLUES

Sunday morning is a day some teach.
For those that are spiritual, it is a day to
preach.
Sunday morning is a day to rest--
From a long hard week, where you did
your best.
For others Sunday may be a day of dread.
The day before work and school, that we
wish won't come we beg.
Sunday is a quiet day a day of silence.
Sunday and everyday should be a day of
non-violence.
Someday Sunday will be a national
Holiday.
But for now we shall focus of what's
happening today.

EXTRA- ORDINARY

Why be normal when you can be extra-
ordinary.
Do something to change the world and
become legendary.
When you do a little more it might be
scary.
Doing more will put you on a road less
traveled but don't be weary.
To be Extra-Ordinary one must go above
and beyond.
That means sticking to a task when others
say so long.
Lastly, I say to you be Extra-Ordinary my
friend.
Keep going above standards until the
very end.

CROOKED SMILE

The goal in life is not to be perfect.
The goal in life is to accomplish what you
thought you couldn't.
When making lines in life don't rely on a
ruler to make it sharp.
But freelance and let your line express the
highs and lows in life, because your smile
is flawed don't hide your teeth.
Be proud, show your smiles and be free.

IN MY FEELINGS

I feel good because I know pain.
I have energy I once was drained.
I am happy now before I was sad.
I love life because I know what I have.
I work hard because I was once doubted.
Success is near my seeds have sprouted.

JOSEPH T. COLLINS AWARD

If you know someone that has integrity
and listens before they speak
If you know someone that has great
knowledge and impresses everyone they
meet
If you know someone who is a very honest
person
If you know someone that is a leader and
very nursing
If you know someone who is very kind
and wise
If you know someone that teaches you
and believes that education is the prize
If you know someone that keeps you
smiling and your never bored
Then that person deserves the Joseph T.
Collins Award

LIONS AND CATS

Lion and cats--
Goals are dreams yet to come.
When you see a mansion remember it
started with a brick.
When you see a finished recipe know it
started with a mix.
These are facts my friend, these are not
tricks.
I am just stating what I know, for I am
not trying to be slick.

EXCUSE ME

Excuse me, but what are your goals?
I thought I would ask to see what you
chose.

SHIPS TO SUCCESS

Your life is a ship the world is the sea.
You will be safe at the dock but you wont
feel free.
You see, ships were made to sail and
explore.
Not play it safe at a dock or a shore.
Ships are made in all different sizes--
And they carry all types of different cargo
and prizes.
Sometimes it's a smooth sail, sometimes
out of the norm.
But ships are made tough to weather the
storm.
Regardless of the destination, regardless
of the cause.
If you are a ship sailing at sea, to you I
applaud.

REFUGEE

Sometimes I feel like I'm not of this
world.
I don't hate people nor do I curse them.
But I love people and wish fortune for all.
Sometimes I feel like a stranger to this
place.
I talk to people and don't ignore them.
I listen to them and realize that they too,
feel like a Refugee.

STOP SIGN

During your journey when you are
traveling the road.
Remember at some point there will be a
stop sign--
Which will delay you from reaching your
destination.
But look both ways to avoid danger and
keep moving forward.

ALONE IN A ROOM

Sometimes I enjoy being alone in a room
My thoughts take me to another place.
I am anyone I want to be.
I am anywhere I can imagine.
Leave me alone in a room.
My thoughts will wonder and—
I shall be back soon.

THE DREAM WAR

Once upon a time I had a dream.
I worked hard, I worked smart, and yes I
screamed.
At times I felt like giving up but I knew I
had to stick to it.
Some nights I would cry but I managed
and got through it.
Many days I was faced with doubt, pain,
and hurt.
But I knew that in order to be successful I
had to continue to work.
Today I will say, my dream is no more.
That is because I made it a reality and I
was able to soar.
I guess you could say, "I won the—
Dream War."

QUESTIONS

It's ok in life if you use your own discretion.
But if problems are too big for you…. it's ok to ask questions.

SUPPORT

Sometimes people just want to know that
you're there.
To some that is the ultimate sign that
shows that you care.
Sometimes people want to feel presence of
others and love.
Presence can give off a feeling of
dedication and love.
Sometimes people just want to know
you're around.
Being reachable is awesome.... even if you
don't make a sound.
Sometimes people want to know that you
will answer when they call.
People just want to know that you will be
there if they fall.

ONE-WAY

In life there are no one-ways.
Which means you can turn around if you
made a bad turn.
You can correct your mistakes and right
your wrong.
In life we get options to choose our path--
And we get skills to master our craft.
So I tell you my friend you will
understand one day.
That on the road through life there is no
one-way.

MISSED OPPORTUNITIES

You miss everything that you don't try.
You should attempt everything and this is
why.
Because you are strong,
Because you are brave,
Because you are wise,
You will save the day.
Because you have integrity,
Because you're a celebrity,
Because you will change the world.
So try it and it won't be any missed
opportunities.

LIGHT UP

Light up yourself,
Light up the room,
Light up the world,
Light up the tombs.
Light up your brain,
Light up your dreams,
Light up hope,
Light up the scene.
Light up ideas,
Light up everywhere,
Could you cut that light on-- that is my
dare.

LOVE ME

Love me when I'm right.
Love me when I'm wrong.
Love me in the night.
Love me when I'm strong.
Love me when I'm scared.
Love me when I'm brave.
Love me when I'm going down the right
path.
Love me till my grave.
Love me deeply.
Don't love me shallow.
Love me like a hawk.
Loves to hunt a sparrow.
Love me when I'm broke.
Love me when I'm rich.
Love me no matter what.
Love me never switch.
Love me!

WAR NO MORE

Here comes a bomb with an answer.
(Boom), There's the bomb, but where's
the answer.
A fact that we never thought about before
If we did…. then war would be no more.

CHOICES AND VOICES

Choices are influenced by voices.
Voices are silenced by choices.
You can make a choice that will be
influenced by a voice—
Or you can let a voice be the deciding
factor for your choice.
Positive voices usually lead to positive
choices.
Choices in the right frame of mind—
Was influenced by positive voices.
Make a choice from a voice because it's
real.
Not a choice from a voice based on how
you feel.

PROBLEM BROOM

I wish I had a broom to sweep away all of
the hurt, my anger, my insecurities, my
bad habits, and my fears.

TAKE OFF

To win a race you must first take off. I
mean how can you finish, if start you—
Didn't cross.

I TRIED

I must do it, so I can say I tried it. I
dream big oceans, you can say I cried it.
My passion for success is huge I can't
deny it. The worst thing that can happen
is I fail and say I tried it.

VOICES

When you hear a voice from within—
That is your very special friend! Listen to
the positive it says, And you are
guaranteed a win.

DON'T PLAY ME

I am not a game.
I am not a sport.
I am not a theatrical play being—
Watched in New York.
I am not an instrument.
I am not a tool.
Don't play me because I am not a fool.

PLANTING SEEDS

Here you are my friend, take these seeds
it's 4, Plant them carefully, step back, and
breathe.
When they begin to grow your dreams
will too.
How do you take care of them you ask?
I'll tell you.
Water them with your love, that's first I
say.
Sunshine will always come from above,
just pray.
Protect them with a fence, people will try
and take it.
Know that there are always copycats.
People will try and make it.
But these are your seeds, which turned
into a garden of success.
That is because you attempted, and tried
your very best.
The 4 seeds; IMAGINE, UNDERSTAND,
PLAN, and EXECUTE. Stay humble,
stay focused, and God will keep blessing
you.

LISTEN

If you listen you will learn a lesson.
But that will lessen if you don't listen.
You will correct your mistakes before
they're made.
If you listen you may even save the day.
People like to talk a lot and listen less.
But those that listen more are the best of
the best.
Besides we all have two ears and one
mouth.
That is so we can listen more to know
what to talk about.

RIGHT PATH

Don't make a left, go to the right path.
The right path is the right path.
The path that has all the possibilities.
The path with more responsibilities.
But you must know with great--
responsibilities come's great power.
And by taking the right path, it will be a
few more hours.
But the right path has no congestion.
It is the right path with all the lessons.
The right path is the right path.

OCEANS

Life is an ocean--
And you are a boat.
Sometimes life is a rapid, sometimes a
mote.

TRUST

Trust must be earned.
Trust makes a team.
Trust is important.
Trust is everything.
Once you lose trust.
Respect may be next.
In order to keep both you must do what's best.
Trust in yourself.
Trust in your dreams.
When you have trust, you can achieve anything.

ORDER IN MY LIFE

In order to bring me down you must first be able to reach me.
In order to criticize me you have to be willing to teach me.
In order to call me a friend you must first show your honesty.
Because to me that is the ultimate sign of loyalty.

MATH CONFLICTS

So you have me now;
Let's add love, subtract hate, and divide
my time to make others great.
Multiply my heart so I have more to give
and that will equal a great life to live.

KEEP MOVING FORWARD

Work hard and good things will come
your way.
Try to do something good for someone
everyday.
The little things in life are what truly
count.
The smallest favors can be the largest
amount.
Showing that you care will make a
persons day.
Showing that you made an effort is the
right and only way.
Volunteer in some way, a thank you
received is great pay.
Whatever you do, just keep moving
forward everyday.

AIRPLANES

I wish that I were on a plane—
To take me away from fear, doubt and—
Pain.
I wish that I were in the sky,
To fly away until I die.
I wish that I were on my way—
To a place where I can enjoy the day.
I wish that I were next to the birds—
And I would look out the window and
make clouds words.
I wish that I were able to fly.
My wings would soar and tears I cry—
But it would be, tears of joy and escaping
the pain.
To me a good day, to others just rain.

SHORT HILLS & TALL DREAMS

"Look, just over that Hill"
See it? Your dream, you've come this far,
and been gone too long to turn back now.
It will take you longer then if you just
continued moving forward.
You are not alone ever, never, physically
nor spiritually.
Come on, pick up your bags and let's
continue to move.
Do this for you to others you have nothing
to prove.
Let's start this climb over this short hill,
And get to the dream so that it will
become real.
I got your back you got my front, so we
are protected.
Once we get to the top of the hill, then we
will respect it.
Now look, behold we are approaching the
top of the hill.
We are closer to a goal born, a moment
with life, a dream you feel.
Once we reach the dream, it is just the
beginning.

The more we dream, the more we work,
and the more we keep winning.
Now we have arrived, we are at the top of
the hill.
Now let us help other people climb, so
they can experience what we feel.
Success flows natural like water down a
stream.
When you concur a Short Hill & a very
Tall Dream.

INDEX

THE
END